Illustrated by
Robin Makowski

Published by Rourke Publishing LLC
Copyright © 2002 Kidsbooks, Inc.

Printed in the USA

Rourke Publishing LLC
Vero Beach, Florida 32964
rourkepublishing.com

Makowski, Robin Lee.
Sea creatures / Robin Lee Makowski
p. cm. — (How to draw)
ISBN 1-58952-156-0
1. Marine animals in art—Juvenile literature. 2. Fish in art—Juvenile literature. 3. Drawing—Technique—Juvenile literature. [1. Marine animals in art. 2. Drawing—Technique.] I. Title. II. How to draw

NC781 .M35 2001
743.6'7—dc21

2001019683

INTRODUCTION

This book will teach you how to draw many different types of sea creatures. Some are more difficult to draw than others, but if you follow along, step by step, you'll soon be able to draw all the sea creatures in this book. You will also learn the methods for drawing anything you want by breaking it down into basic shapes.

The most basic and commonly used shape is the oval. There are many variations of ovals—some are small and round, others are long and flat, and many are in between.

Most of the figures in this book begin with some kind of oval. Then, other ovals, shapes, and lines are added to form the basic outline of a sea creature.

Many times a free-form oval is used, like the ones pictured below. In addition to ovals, variations of other basic shapes, such as circles, squares, rectangles, triangles, and simple lines are used to connect the shapes. Using these basic shapes will help you start your drawing.

Some basic oval shapes:

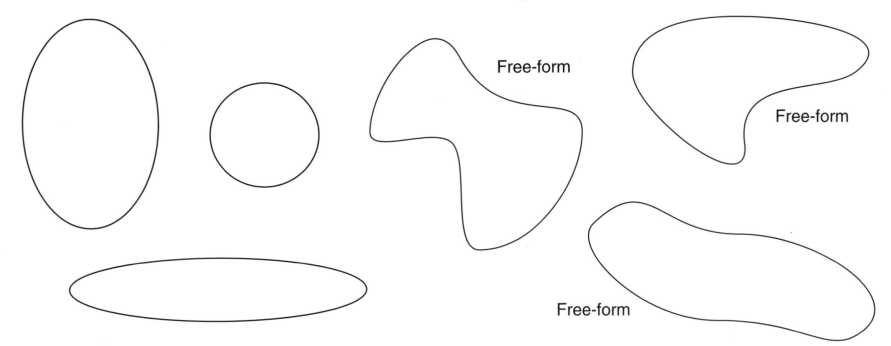

Free-form

Free-form

Free-form

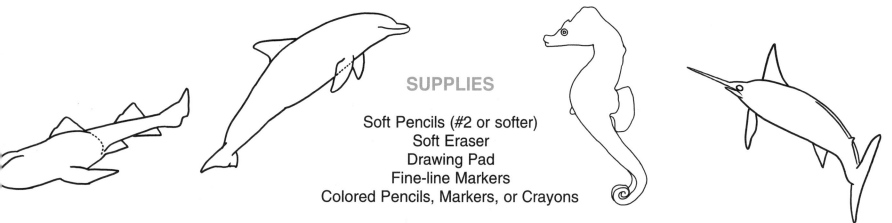

SUPPLIES

Soft Pencils (#2 or softer)
Soft Eraser
Drawing Pad
Fine-line Markers
Colored Pencils, Markers, or Crayons

HELPFUL HINTS

1. Following steps 1 and 2 carefully will make the final steps easier. The first two steps create a solid foundation for the figure—much like a builder who must first construct a foundation before building the rest of the house. Next comes the fun part—creating the smooth, clean outline of the animal, and adding all the finishing touches and color.

2. Always keep your pencil lines light and soft. These "guidelines" will be easier to erase when you no longer need them.

3. Don't be afraid to erase. It usually takes a lot of drawing and erasing before you will be satisfied with the way your drawing looks.

4. Add details, shading, and all the finishing touches after you have blended and refined all the shapes and your figure is complete.

5. Remember: Practice Makes Perfect. Don't be discouraged if you can't get the hang of it right away. Just keep drawing and erasing until you do.

HOW TO START

Look below at the drawing of the sea turtle, and study it. Then study the steps it took to get to the final drawing. Note how the shapes overlap and where they intersect.

1. Start with a lightly drawn, free-form oval for the body. Add ovals for the head, the back flippers, and a free-form oval for the front flipper.

2. Shape the head, forming the beak, mouth, and eye. Add the other flipper under the chin. Define the shell, and round and smooth the flippers.

3. Draw the scales on the shell, head, and flippers. Leave the left, back flipper unscaled, as it will be completely in shadow. Draw the wrinkles on the neck.

4. Add the detailed shading. It looks complicated, but this animal is one of the easiest to draw realistically.

Remember: It's not important to get it perfect. It is important for you to be happy with your work!

Erasing Tips
● Once you have completed the outline, erase your guidelines. Then proceed to shading and/or coloring your drawing.
● Using a permanent, fine-line marker over the pencil guidelines you wish to keep, will make it easier to erase the pencil lines you no longer need.
● A very soft or kneaded eraser will erase the pencil lines without smudging the drawing or ripping the paper.

Most of all, HAVE FUN!

1.

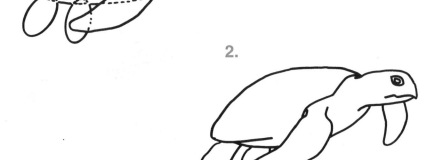

2.

3.

4.

Lesser Electric Ray

If touched, the fifteen-inch lesser electric eel can deliver a mild electric shock, about enough to light up a 50-watt light bulb. Found from North Carolina to Argentina, the ray is tan with smoky-brown fins and markings. This relative of the shark is best avoided!

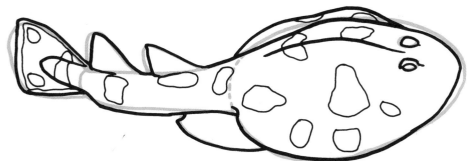

2. Form and smooth the body and erase any overlapping lines. Then add the irregular spots all over the body and tail.

1. Draw a free-form oval for the body and connect it to the triangular tail by a long, thin tail stalk. Draw the fins on the tail and two ovals for the eyes.

3. Add details and shading for the finishing touches. Make the edge of the spots dark and centers a little lighter. Leave a white edge around the ray as you add the shading.

Orca

The distinctive black and white orca is the largest member of the dolphin family. Most spend their entire life in the family group, or pod, into which they were born. Each pod has its own dialect, or "accent" in communicating with its members. Playful, acrobatic orcas are found in all oceans, though they prefer colder waters.

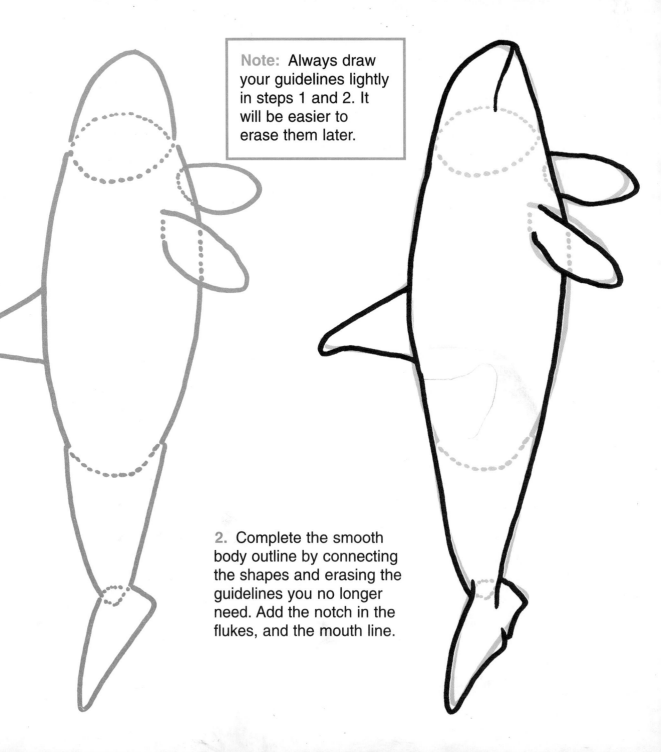

Note: Always draw your guidelines lightly in steps 1 and 2. It will be easier to erase them later.

1. Begin with a large oval for the body, two smaller ovals for the pec fins, a gumdrop shape for the head, and a cone shape for the tail stalk. Add triangles for the tall dorsal fin and tail flukes.

2. Complete the smooth body outline by connecting the shapes and erasing the guidelines you no longer need. Add the notch in the flukes, and the mouth line.

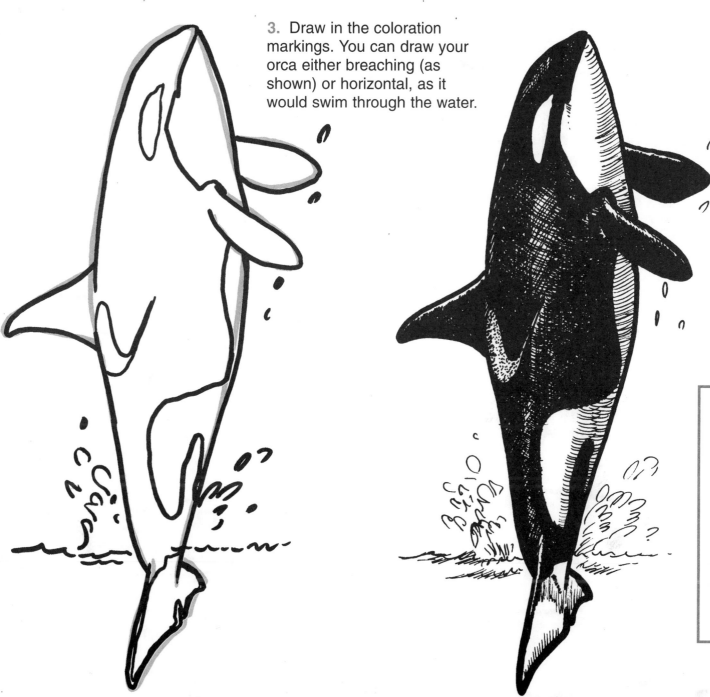

3. Draw in the coloration markings. You can draw your orca either breaching (as shown) or horizontal, as it would swim through the water.

4. Complete the drawing by adding cross-hatched shading. Can you see the eye between the the front of the eye patch and the the mouth line? When you're finished, draw a pod of orcas swimming together.

Crosshatching is simply parallel and/or intersecting lines through the areas to be shaded. A light area of shade would have light, thin lines with more space between them; darker shading would show thicker, closer lines and more intersecting (crossing) lines.

Great Barracuda

Growing to six feet, the shiny, silver great barracuda lives in warm seas. Boasting an impressive set of teeth, these barracuda are awesome predators in their reef habitats. As scary as they look, they are usually not a threat to humans.

1. Begin by lightly drawing a long, surfboard-shaped oval. Add triangular shapes for the tail and fins. Draw the mouth with a line, and the eye with a circle.

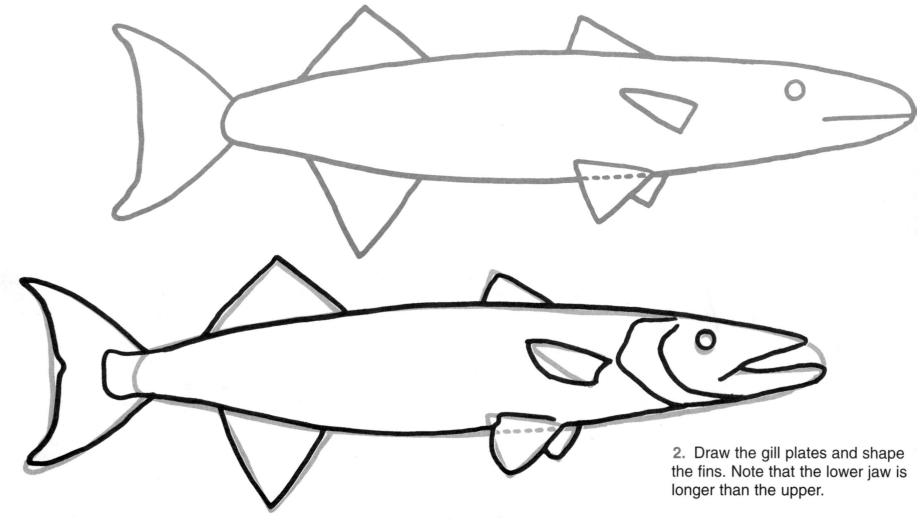

2. Draw the gill plates and shape the fins. Note that the lower jaw is longer than the upper.

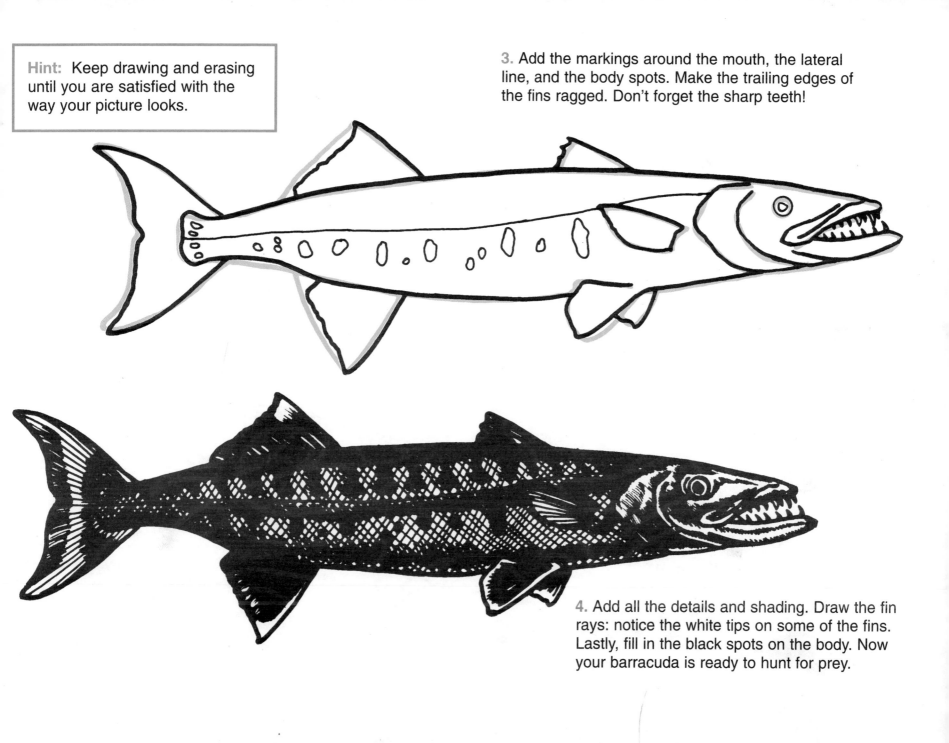

3. Add the markings around the mouth, the lateral line, and the body spots. Make the trailing edges of the fins ragged. Don't forget the sharp teeth!

4. Add all the details and shading. Draw the fin rays: notice the white tips on some of the fins. Lastly, fill in the black spots on the body. Now your barracuda is ready to hunt for prey.

Blue Shark

Common in the colder Pacific waters, the blue shark grows to twelve feet. Blue-gray above and white below, the shark's coloration protects it in its deep-ocean habitat.

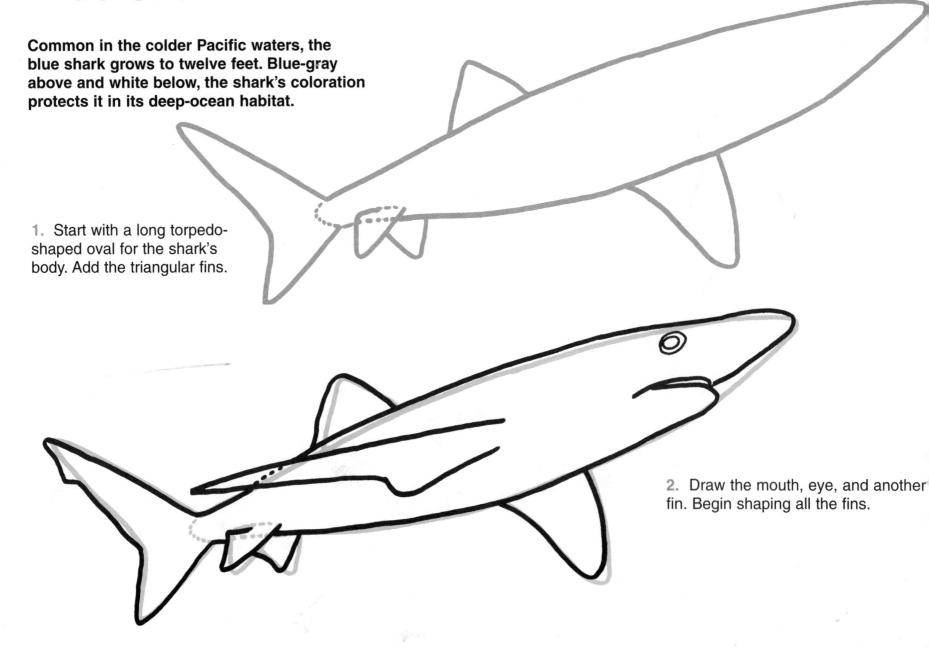

1. Start with a long torpedo-shaped oval for the shark's body. Add the triangular fins.

2. Draw the mouth, eye, and another fin. Begin shaping all the fins.

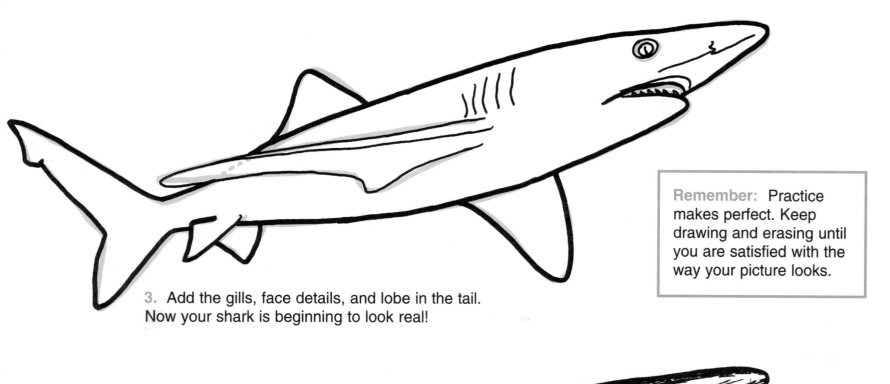

3. Add the gills, face details, and lobe in the tail. Now your shark is beginning to look real!

4. Complete your blue shark by adding shading. The color on the belly is shadow, since the shark actually has a white belly and white under its fins. Don't forget to darken the eye.

Gafftopsail Catfish

Named for the long spines on its dorsal and pectoral fins, this catfish can grow to over three feet. Its pointy, sharp spines can cause painful wounds to humans. The fish is blue-gray above, fading to silvery sides and white belly.

1. Draw a long, missile-shaped oval for the body. Attach a free-form oval for the head, and create the "V"-shaped tail. Note that the top part of the tail is longer than the lower.

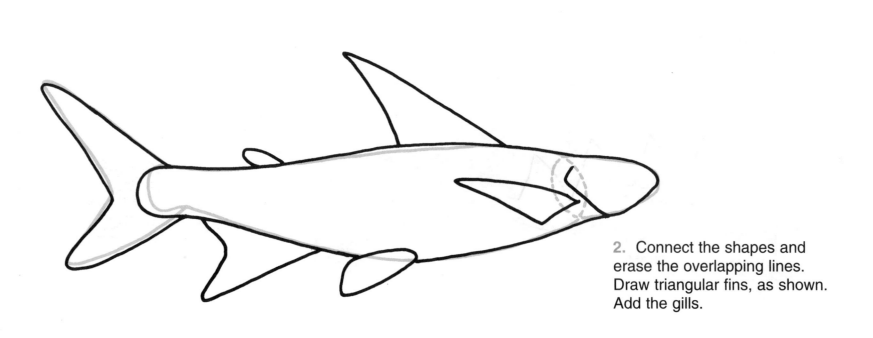

2. Connect the shapes and erase the overlapping lines. Draw triangular fins, as shown. Add the gills.

3. Sketch the eye, the long barbels (whiskers), and the spikes from the dorsal and pectoral fins. Draw the lateral line and begin shaping the fins.

Note: Before going to step 4, make sure you are satisfied with the way your drawing looks.

4. Draw the fin rays and add details and shading. The gafftopsail catfish is a sociable fish that lives in large groups, so draw a school of them!

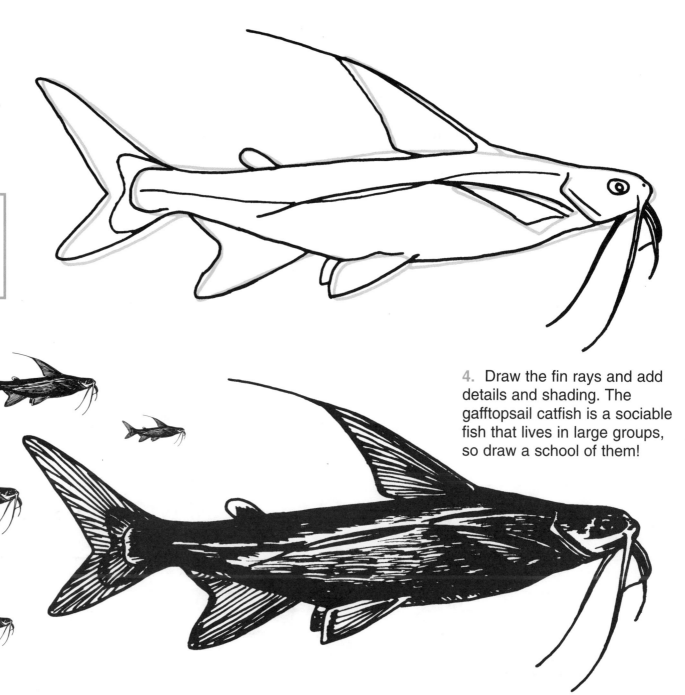

Blue Whale

The blue whale is the largest animal to ever inhabit the earth. It can be found in most temperate and polar seas, growing to over 100 feet and weighing up to 300,000 pounds! Blue whales are slate blue above and lighter below, with large, long spots and blotches covering the back and flanks.

Note: Keep your guide-lines lightly drawn.

Indent slightly

1. Begin with a huge, pointed free-form shape, about four times longer than it is wide. At the right end, draw a long, flat triangle for the flukes.

2. Draw the mouth and eye, dipping the curve of the mouth down. Add the pectoral fin in line with the eye and mouth. Draw the tiny dorsal fin and begin shaping the flukes. Slightly indent the top of the head (this is where the blowholes are).

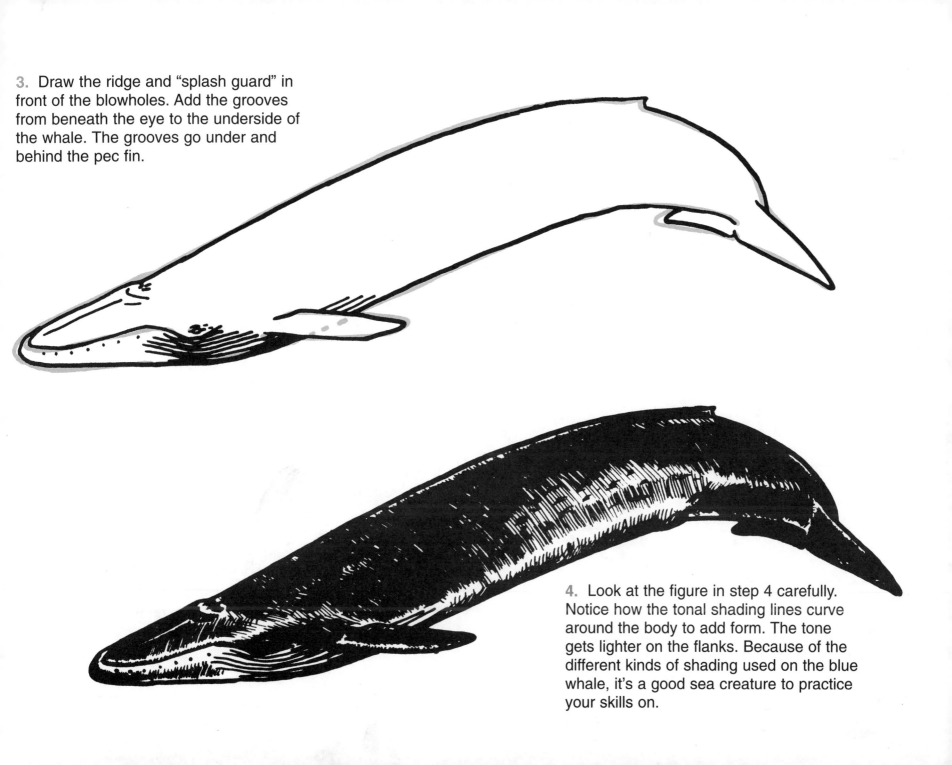

3. Draw the ridge and "splash guard" in front of the blowholes. Add the grooves from beneath the eye to the underside of the whale. The grooves go under and behind the pec fin.

4. Look at the figure in step 4 carefully. Notice how the tonal shading lines curve around the body to add form. The tone gets lighter on the flanks. Because of the different kinds of shading used on the blue whale, it's a good sea creature to practice your skills on.

Peacock Flounder

A strange thing happens to a flounder as it matures—
its right eye moves over to the left side of its head
so that it can lie flat on the bottom of the ocean! Able
to camouflage itself by changing colors, the peacock
flounder not only finds protection in its reef home,
but "hides" in the open from prey. Peacock flounders
grow to eighteen inches and have blue ring markings
and dots.

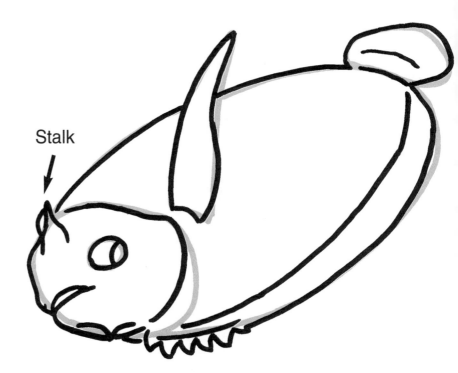

Stalk

2. Draw a stalk with the partially visible other eye. Add
lightly drawn guidelines for the gill plate, mouth, and ventral
fin. Note that the ventral fin goes across the entire bottom
of the fish, and has a pointed section under the chin.

1. Begin with a large oval for the body. Add a smaller oval
within for the head, and ovals for the eye and tail. A spiky
pectoral fin sticks up as the fish lays on its side.

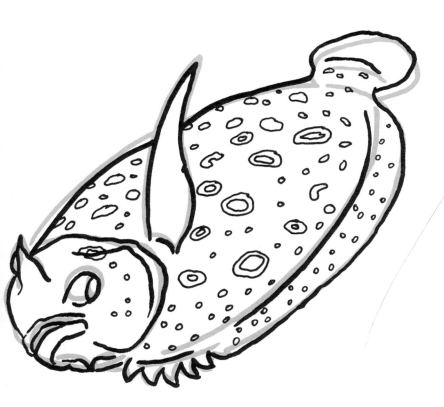

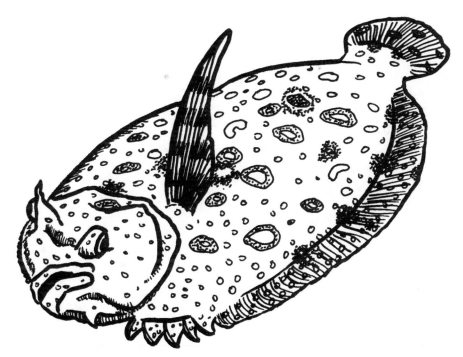

4. Draw the fin rays and all other details to the peacock flounder. Then hide it on the sandy sea bottom.

3. Blend all the shapes together, erasing unneeded lines as you go along. Add the ringed markings and details to the face.

Bottlenose Dolphin

Growing to thirteen feet, the playful bottlenose dolphin is found in all temperate and tropical oceans. Though colored gray above, the dolphin's light belly often blushes pink when it gets angry or excited.

1. Begin with a large, lightly drawn oval guideline for the body. Add an egg shape for the head, and a long, free-form for the tail stalk. Triangles of different shapes form the snout, tail flukes, and dorsal fin.

2. Smooth and combine the body shapes and erase the overlapping lines. Form the flukes, the rostrum (beak), and the trademark "smile." Add the pectoral fins.

3. Add the eye just above and behind the corner of the mouth. Shape the dorsal and pec fins.

4. Now add the texture. Curve some of your crosshatch shading lines around to give dimension to the form. Shading gives your drawing a realistic look. It may be hard to get it right in the beginning, but if you keep at it you will be pleased with the final results.

Deep-Sea Anglerfish

Living deep in the ocean where light never penetrates, the deep-sea anglerfish is undetectable except for its lighted lure. The lure attracts prey towards the angler-fish's transparent teeth.

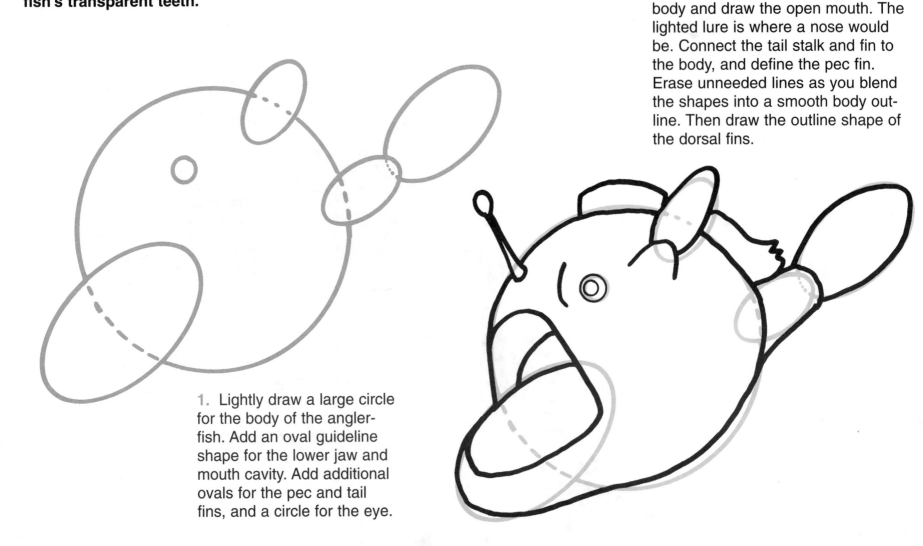

2. Connect the "jaw" oval to the body and draw the open mouth. The lighted lure is where a nose would be. Connect the tail stalk and fin to the body, and define the pec fin. Erase unneeded lines as you blend the shapes into a smooth body outline. Then draw the outline shape of the dorsal fins.

1. Lightly draw a large circle for the body of the angler-fish. Add an oval guideline shape for the lower jaw and mouth cavity. Add additional ovals for the pec and tail fins, and a circle for the eye.

4. Detail the anglerfish by following the contour of its body with your shading lines. Draw the fin rays. For the finishing touch, leave the pupil bright and the teeth transparent (do this by making the inside of the mouth dark). Now your anglerfish is ready for some dinner.

3. Draw the sharp, raggedy teeth. Spike the first few dorsal fins, making the outlines of the other fins ragged. Start adding details as you continue to smooth and refine the angler's outline shape.

Hint: Breaking down complicated areas into simple shapes makes them easier to draw.

Hawksbill Sea Turtle

This endangered marine reptile can reach a length of three feet. Sea turtles spend their entire life at sea, with the females coming on land only to lay their eggs in the sand. Hawksbill sea turtles have a dark, patterned top shell and a yellow bottom shell. The scales on their flippers and head are reddish brown above and yellow-white below.

1. Start with a lightly drawn, free-form oval for the body. Add ovals for the head, the back flippers, and a free-form oval for the front flipper.

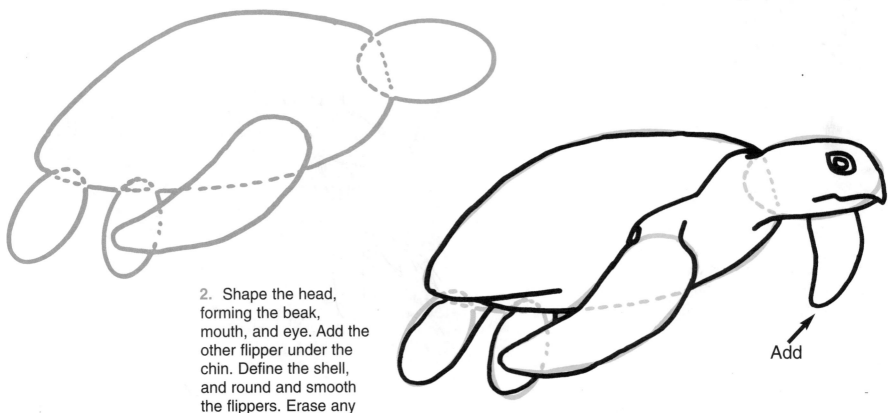

2. Shape the head, forming the beak, mouth, and eye. Add the other flipper under the chin. Define the shell, and round and smooth the flippers. Erase any overlapping lines.

Add

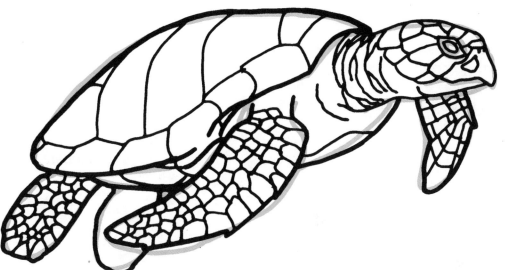

3. Draw the scales on the shell, head, and flippers. Leave the left, back flipper unscaled, as it will be completely in shadow. Draw the wrinkles on the neck.

Pro Tip:
For realistic-looking scales:
a) Draw the flipper scales in light, soft pencil.
b) Outline the flipper (not the scales!) with a permanent, fine-line marker.
c) Color the inside of the scales up to the pencil lines. Do not color over the pencil lines.
d) Gently erase the pencil lines. The scales will remain and look naturally outlined. This trick works for fish scales and bird feathers, too!

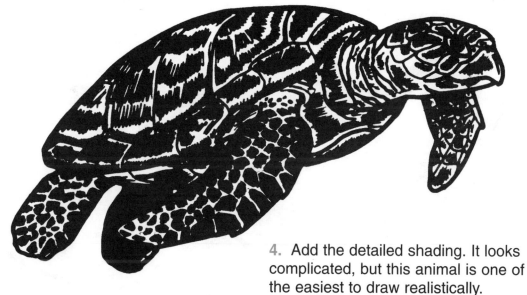

4. Add the detailed shading. It looks complicated, but this animal is one of the easiest to draw realistically.

Octopus

The shy reef octopus is a member of a large family of octopuses which range in size from a couple of inches to several feet. Octopuses change color and even grow warts to suit their emotional state. Color change helps camouflage them from predators. The 20-inch reef octopus's color varies, but it usually has a blue-green background with rust-colored mottling.

1. Begin with two overlapping guideline ovals for the head and body. Add circles for the eyes, and add a "hood" over the left eye.

2. Slowly and carefully, one line at a time, draw the legs. Notice how they curl around. Erase any unnecessary guidelines.

3. Draw the flat bottom on each tentacle and note the curls. Draw the markings, paying attention to the curve of the arms and head.

> **Remember:** Keep drawing and erasing until you've got it just right.

4. Create the suction cups on the legs by drawing two tiny circles next to each other. Finish your octopus by completing the shading. This drawing will really give you a sense of accomplishment!

Sea Horse

The sea horse lives in all temperate and tropical oceans. It comes in a variety of colors and patterns. Many sea horses are colored to match the corals and plants they hang on to as they feed on plankton.

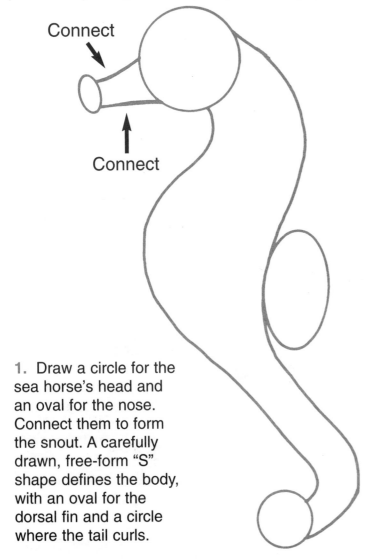

Connect

Connect

2. Combine, blend, and define the shapes. Form the head, add the eye, curl the tip of the tail, and shape the dorsal fin.

1. Draw a circle for the sea horse's head and an oval for the nose. Connect them to form the snout. A carefully drawn, free-form "S" shape defines the body, with an oval for the dorsal fin and a circle where the tail curls.

Note: Only go to step 3 after you are satisfied with the ouline of the sea horse you have just drawn. Don't be intimidated by the complicated design of the sea horse. Remember to take it one shape at a time.

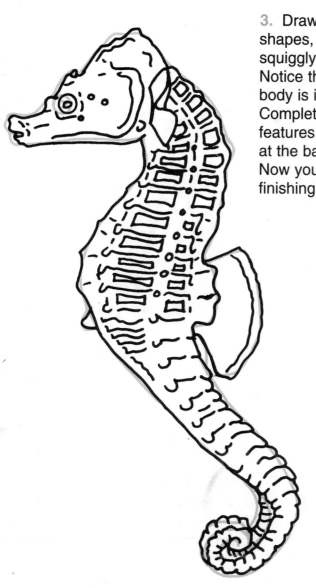

3. Draw the rectanglular shapes, tiny circles, and squiggly lines all over the body. Notice that the ouline of the body is indented or "rippled." Complete the head and facial features, adding the pectoral fin at the back of the head. Now you're ready for the finishing touches.

4. Add the fin rays and detail the sea horse. Patches of shading, as shown, will create a realistic look. Shading can be loose. Don't worry about staying within the lines!

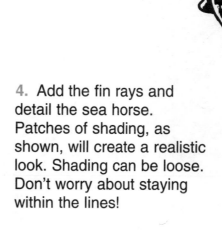

Swordfish

One of the most sought-after game fish, the broadbill swordfish is silvery gray, with an unusually large eye that gives it a startled appearance. It lives in coastal waters in both the Atlantic and Pacific oceans. The tall dorsal and pectoral fins, fixed in place, distinguish this billfish from others.

1. Start by sketching a large, banana-shaped guideline oval. At one end attach a small oval for the head. At the other, add the tail stalk and tail.

2. Blend and smooth the outline into the fish's overall shape. Erase the overlapping lines. Create the head, adding the long bill, mouth, and eye. Lastly, add the fins. Now you're ready to add the details that will make your drawing look finished.

3. Draw the gills and refine the facial details. Shape the fins and add the lateral line.

4. Complete the swordfish by drawing the fin rays. Then, crosshatch the dark back, blending to lighter on the sides.

Horn Shark

The four-foot horn shark has a white belly and a golden brown back dotted with dark spots. A sharp spine, or horn, sticks up at the base of each dorsal fin. This shark lives in the Pacific, from Central California to the Sea of Cortez. It feeds on crustaceans, which it grinds up with its large, flat teeth. Horn sharks are relatively harmless, and they are frequently kept in aquariums.

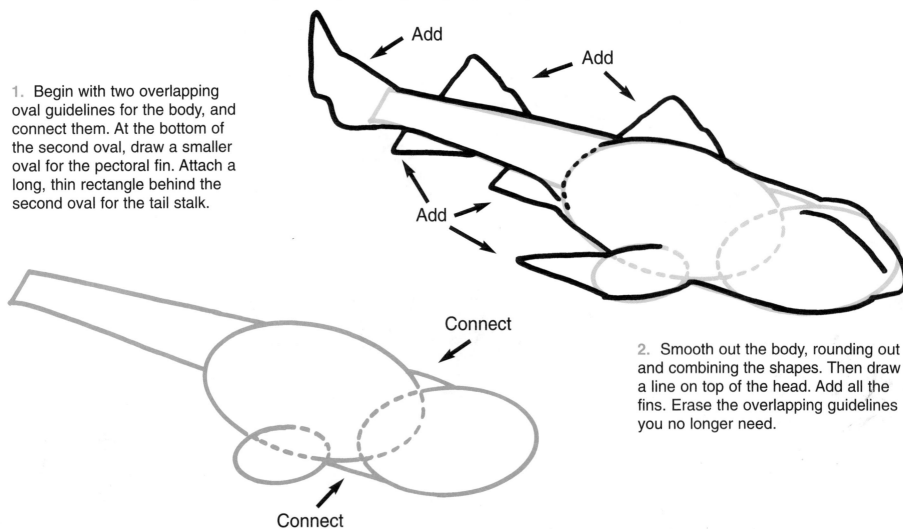

1. Begin with two overlapping oval guidelines for the body, and connect them. At the bottom of the second oval, draw a smaller oval for the pectoral fin. Attach a long, thin rectangle behind the second oval for the tail stalk.

Add

Add

Add

Connect

Connect

2. Smooth out the body, rounding out and combining the shapes. Then draw a line on top of the head. Add all the fins. Erase the overlapping guidelines you no longer need.

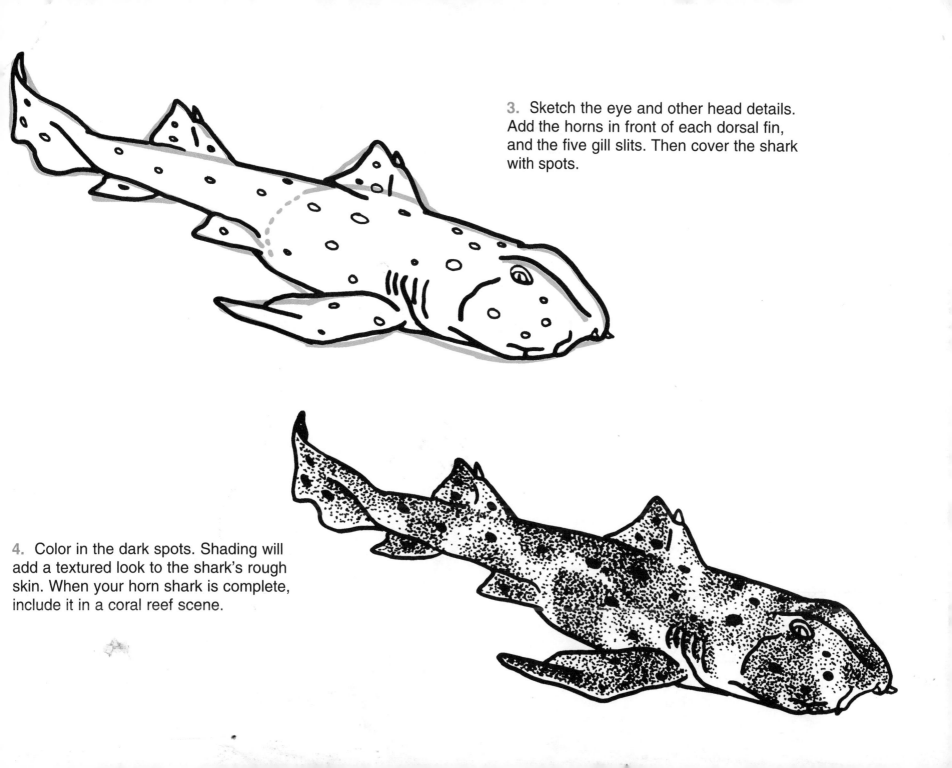

3. Sketch the eye and other head details. Add the horns in front of each dorsal fin, and the five gill slits. Then cover the shark with spots.

4. Color in the dark spots. Shading will add a textured look to the shark's rough skin. When your horn shark is complete, include it in a coral reef scene.

Elephant Seal

A male elephant seal, called a bull, is an impressive sight! Named for his long nose, the bull can rear up to fight other males with canine teeth. This shiny, reddish-tan giant can grow to eighteen feet. Elephant seals are found in temperate to polar oceans and spend the entire year, except for breeding time, at sea.

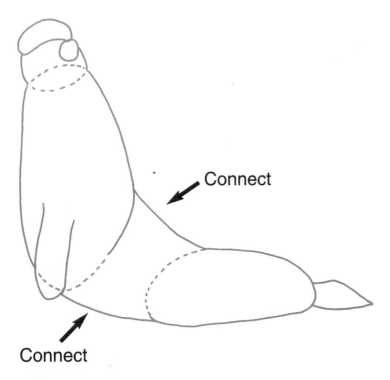

Connect

Connect

1. Draw two free-form ovals for the main body sections and connect them. Add a small oval for the head, and a fat hot-dog shape for the large nose. Add the ear and flipper shapes.

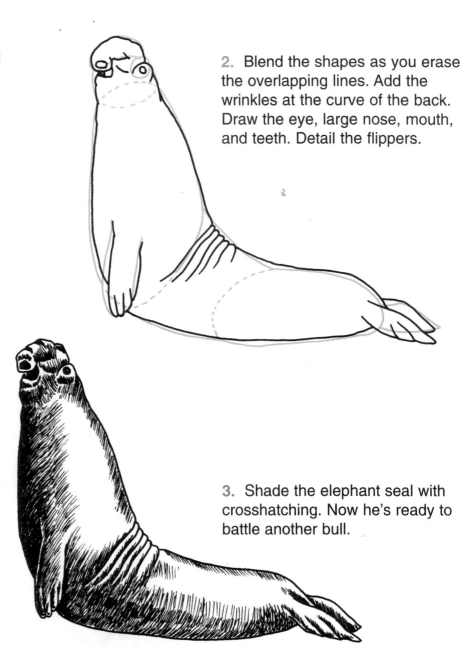

2. Blend the shapes as you erase the overlapping lines. Add the wrinkles at the curve of the back. Draw the eye, large nose, mouth, and teeth. Detail the flippers.

3. Shade the elephant seal with crosshatching. Now he's ready to battle another bull.